Praise for *The Secret Life of the Corporate Jester*

"*The Secret Life of the Corporate Jester* is refreshing. The writing is crisp and clear and it doesn't just teach, but builds suspense and poses questions for the reader to ponder. This book will quickly change your perspective on managing and leading. Every person that wants to influence culture change and build leadership in any organization should give this a read."

> *Doug Bryant, Vice President, Organizational Development, Advance Auto Parts*

"Awesome! I loved it ... a good read ... really different and magical ... would consider using it as a leadership training experience."

> *Merrill Adragna, Manager for Employee Communications, Meetings, Events and Recognition at one of the nation's leading financial services companies*

"*The Secret Life of the Corporate Jester* is a fun and intriguing read filled with insights into what it takes to be a successful leader in today's complex corporate environments. I love the entertaining way the story unfolds, holding your attention and interest as it leads you through self discovery, revealing the path to forward your own leadership development. It's a great book!"

> *Mary Peery, Senior Vice President, Strategic Change Management, Hewlett Packard*

"The concept offered a realistic way to overcome leadership shortcomings. The writing style successfully leads the reader through a learning process. I could see this as a successful training tool. I liked it!"

> *Dean Parker, Senior Vice President, Marketing, Great Central Insurance Company, Member of the Argonaut Group*

"I truly enjoyed the book and think it would be a valuable edition to any leader's bookshelf. Developing an ability to eliminate blind spots, our own or those of others, is essential for success in every business."

> *David Steinhart, Learning Consultant, Leadership, Development and Training, Pratt & Whitney Rocketdyne*

"...a totally unique and really outstanding way for the reader to look at organizational culture and leadership."

> *William Cooper,* **Reader Views**

"The reality is that most of us are afraid to disagree with the status quo and really get to the truth of what needs to be changed in our workplace and in our lives. *The Secret Life of the Corporate Jester* explores this very interesting concept. Think what we could all do with such skills, both in our workplace and in our lives in general."

Tami Brady, **TCM Reviews**

"A great and on-target read. I recommend it for mid- and high-level managers who want to improve the leadership they contribute to their organizations."

Terri Thorson, Principal, **PR Connection**

"Most business books sell a methodology of management—a way of doing things. In reality, one size doesn't fit all. *Corporate Jester* isn't a way of operating, but a way of thinking—a paradigm of openness and a way to achieve it."

Jim Karger, **Why Work Isn't Working Anymore — 3 Tools To Transform Your Workplace As If People Mattered**

"*The Secret Life of the Corporate Jester* is an easy read for every leader in every type of organization that wants to make a positive difference. This book inspires you to make good things happen. It is a must read for anyone who wants to achieve greater success."

Laura Cassidy, Manager, Leadership Development, Northrop Grumman Information Technology Learning & Development

"Too many corporate bosses are surrounded by sycophantic yes men and women who are not doing their organization any favors by saying the things their bosses want to hear. The author has produced a helpful management how-to that gives many practical suggestions on how to influence corporate organizational improvement. He has translated a role from feudal pasts into a useful tool for organizational effectiveness."

Bob Spear, Head Reviewer, **Heartland Reviews**

"In the great Irish tradition of the bard, corporate jesters can speak truth to power without losing their heads. David's book is an excellent, tightly written introduction to the idea that there are more ways to move a company forward than endless brainstorming meetings in the executive suite. Sometimes the Big Cheese just needs to hear the unadorned facts."

Frank O'Mahony, NVNG, Inc., and former corporate spokesman for Apple Computer

The Secret Life of the Corporate Jester

A FRESH PERSPECTIVE ON ORGANIZATIONAL LEADERSHIP, CULTURE AND BEHAVIOR

The Secret Life of the CORPORATE JESTER

David T. Riveness

Jardin Publishing

Copyright David T. Riveness, 2006. Printed and bound in the United States by Jardin Publishing. All rights reserved. Without limiting the rights under copyright reserved above, no part of this publication may be reproduced, stored in or introduced into a retrieval system, or transmitted in any form or by any means (electronic, mechanical, photocopying, recording or otherwise), except by a reviewer who may quote brief passages in a review to be published in a newspaper or magazine, without the prior written permission of both the author and the publisher of this book. For more information, contact Jardin Publishing at info@jardinpublishing.com.

ATTENTION CORPORATIONS, UNIVERSITIES AND PROFESSIONAL ORGANIZATIONS: Special discounts on bulk quantities of this book for educational, training or gift purposes are available. Special editions can be created to fit specific needs or events. For details, contact info@jardinpublishing.com.

Library of Congress Control Number: 2005910976

First Edition, printed 2006

www.corporatejester.com
www.jardinpublishing.com

Dedication and Acknowledgments

This work is dedicated with enthusiasm to all who have been jesters for me: family, friends, teachers, students, colleagues and clients. Who I am today is the sum total of the influences you had on me along my journey.

Special thanks to my family—John and Sylvia Riveness, Kevin and Deborah Linggi, and Grandma Gerson.

More thanks to Jim Karger, Colin Campbell, Talisa Ernstmann, The Goyettes, Sue Krautkramer, Dana Hansen, Melissa Dragich-Cordero, Scott Carter, Jennifer Schmidt, David Garza, all of my friends at Eagle's Flight, Doug Bryant, John Edwards, Dean Parker, Mary Peery, Frank Rogers-Witte, Cathi Stevenson, Merrill Adragna, David Steinhart, Terri Thorson, Laura Cassidy, and Frank O'Mahony.

Additional thanks to the people in San Miguel de Allende, Mexico, who offered advice and encouragement over cups of coffee.

Author's Note:

Many people have heard of the story of the starfish on the beach, but it bears repeating here because it speaks to the heart of jestership.

One day, a man was walking along the beach, watching the ocean waves breaking on the shore, when he turned a corner and noticed a most unusual thing. He saw this part of the beach was littered with thousands of starfish that had washed up on shore and were dying in the sun. Far down the beach in the distance, he could see a woman picking up starfish and throwing them back into the ocean, one after another. When he was close enough to speak to her, he said, "You are wasting your time. There are thousands of starfish here. You can't possibly make a difference." The woman stared at the man and reached down to pick up a starfish and flung it back into the sea. "I made a difference for that one," she said, and reached down to pick up another.

You will find that jestership requires commitment to a unique relationship with those around you. At times, this may be difficult to maintain . . . keeping that level of commitment with a smile on your face may seem monumentally hard. Look at each opportunity to provide jestership as it comes, one starfish at a time, and you will be on your way to making a difference in your organization.

Contents

The First Email
1

The Story of the Early Jesters
8

The Mystery of Blind Spots
16

Human Behavior and the Abilene Paradox
20

Uncovering Examples of Real World Jesters
23

The Delivery of the Handbook
34

Snow White, Mirror Measurement and Self Delusion
38

Communication, Understanding and an Ancient Stone
41

Promotion, Hesitation and the Sword of Damocles
45

Lost History, Atlantis and Reinventing the Wheel
49

The Olympic Flame and Personal Branding
53

Icarus, Overconfidence and Organizational Insight
56

The Cat, the Fox and Commitment to Lifelong Learning
59

Statements of Mission, Blind Men and an Elephant
63

Leader Identification, Hidden Talent and the Sword in the Stone
66

Spoken Word, Gutenberg Bible and Organizational Communication
70

The Old Man, Personal Ethics and the Scorpion
74

Hercules, Hero Creation and Organizational Training
77

Corporate Vulnerability and the Weakness of Achilles
80

Creating and Furthering Jestership in Your World
87

An Invitation
93

The first e-mail appeared on a rainy Friday afternoon and was entirely unexpected. In hindsight, it came at the perfect time, but I would not understand why for months. I now mark time in only two ways: before that first e-mail arrived ... and after.

I remember returning home from a session with a client and checking my e-mail. Nestled among the ads for dubious products I would never want and dating sites I would never visit was a singularly curious message. I almost sent it to the junk mail folder because I didn't recognize the return address, challenge@corporatejester.com. The subject line caught my eye, though: "Leadership ... how are you contributing?" My finger hovered over the Delete button as my mind registered the words. My line of work! I opened the e-mail.

Dave ... are you doing **everything** *you can to help people develop into better leaders? I suspect you know you aren't.*

No signature.

My first reaction was not a positive one. In fact, I was a little offended. Over the past 8 years I had worked as a facilitator—an "organizational consultant" to use a fancier term. I had built a career out of advising countless individuals, companies, and organizations on a great variety of topics relating to organizational and individual success.

As the years ticked by, I used my backstage pass into corporate America to learn and understand more and more about how organizations operated and how people behaved within them. I learned to look at each new assignment as a peek into the behavior of people trying to unlock the secrets of success. Warner Bros., NIKE,

ESPN, Pfizer, The American Heart Association, Citibank; as the list grew larger I slowly added to my body of knowledge. At this point in my life I was confident I knew a little something about leadership!

I assumed the e-mail was a prank sent by one of my friends to poke fun. It was curious, though. I checked out www.corporatejester.com to see whether there was a website associated with the sender's address. A site did come up, but nothing was displayed except a "coming soon" banner. Hmmm. Ok, I thought, I'll play along.

I clicked back to my e-mail program and typed: *I suspect I know more about leadership than you ever will! Want to take a look my résumé?*

I thought about my work as I waited for a response. The vast majority of people I spoke to wanted to be more successful, happier, and better "leaders." As I traveled from organization to organization I noticed that leadership development continued to be a holy grail in both private and public sectors. People wanted to see exceptional leadership clearly exhibited in their management, their staff, and their peers. Middle managers craved to be perceived as true leaders and true leaders wished everyone in their organization could truly understand and embrace the concept.

A quiet beep from my computer pulled me out of my thoughts. A response.

I have seen your résumé. Impressive, but it really doesn't speak to your **potential***. Your contribution to others is not to be found in the knowledge you have accumulated, or the numbers of people you have spoken in front of, but in who you have decided to* **be** *for others in the world. By the way, we might have to work a little on your ego.*

I didn't know exactly what to make of this. I hadn't been so boldly challenged in a long time. I wasn't sure whether I liked it. I quickly typed back:

Who exactly are you? What right do you have to judge my contribution? And what do you mean by "who I have decided to **be** *for others in the world"?*

I waited by the computer for an hour or so, but no answer appeared.

That night, I thought a little about the curious e-mails. I realized that if I let go of my ego for a second, I could see that my new pen pal had a point. To be honest, recently I had started to question the level of my contribution to others.

On paper my job was to provide insight into leadership issues that were troubling individuals and organizations. Over the years, as I improved my ability to uncover behaviors that created success (as well as those that led to failure), I began to notice something fascinating. The similarity between the issues that individuals and organizations wrestled with were striking. Over and over, I encountered the same roadblocks to success. In each case, the solution, while clearer to me, remained hidden from the people involved. Blind spots in their thinking kept them from recognizing critical information, powerful choices, and clear paths to follow. What was my contribution to these people?

I thought again about the e-mail. Who am I for others in the world? Pretty intense question. Interesting to think about. I lay in bed that evening wondering about the answer. Tossing and turning, I finally fell into a restless sleep realizing I didn't really know.

The next day, I had forgotten about the previous night's e-mails; I had all the other things on my mind that make up a workday. Later in the morning I finally got to my computer and noticed another message from my new, mysterious friend sitting in my in-box. I clicked it open:

I'm a jester. And so are you ... you just don't know it yet. When you understand this you will understand your true potential to contribute.

Now that didn't make much sense. A jester? I know that I can be funny, and I typically create relationships based on fun and humor. Truthfully, I have always been a bit of a class clown. But a jester? I didn't get it. I often worked with serious organizations that preferred a serious, traditional suit-and-tie attitude. Clowning around would not be acceptable. What could jesters have to do with them? I typed back:

Funny. Do I have to go out and buy a pointy, multicolored hat? Listen, in the real world of leadership there is no place for jesters. It is serious business!

I figured my sarcastic response might end the conversation, but immediately received a reply:

Smile. Certainly you can buy a hat, if it helps you get in the right mood. But I'm not really talking about the kind of jester you're thinking about ... bells and colorful costumes and juggling. I'm talking about the concept of jestership ... the relationship of jesters to those around them. Do you know the **true** *history of the jester?*

Interesting. That response had come back fast. Whoever was e-mailing me was online now. This was turning into a real-time conversation. I typed back:

Not really. My only knowledge of jesters comes from the clowns I have seen in movies about medieval England.

The response popped back:

I think you will find the real history of jesters to be much more interesting ... and much more applicable to you. Tell me what you think after you read the attached. Let me know if you want to hear more.

Attached to the e-mail was a scan of something that looked like a page out of a lined notebook that had run through the washing machine a couple of times. It appeared to be quite old. I made out faint outlines of fold marks and some Asian-looking characters scrawled in the margin. I didn't know it yet, but I would come to love the mysterious attachments that frequently were attached to the e-mails.

I squinted at the faint type and started reading:

Hung-wu was a very important person in Chinese history. He became emperor of China in 1368 and founded the Ming dynasty that ruled China for nearly 300 years. When Hung-wu became emperor he proceeded to make some changes in the way the government ran. He felt that past leaders had allowed too much freedom in the local provinces, so he began to centralize power (militarily, administratively and educationally) back into the imperial government under his control. As a result, he began to try to conduct state affairs by himself. Soon after, he found that the daily mountain of work proved too much for one man to handle … even for an emperor. To assist him, he appointed several loyal mid-level officials to new positions, creating a large body designed to advise him and increase his ability to run the government. He expected the advisors to gather vast amounts of information, summarize it, and then report it back to him in a condensed version to be used in his deliberations. Although he ended up farming out most of the day-to-day information gathering to his body of advisors, he always reserved final decisions in state affairs for himself. This system caught on and was eventually copied by the lesser governments in the 15 provinces that existed at the time.

Each of those provinces had its own mini version of an emperor ... a regional governor whose role was to render judgment on matters that were deemed not important enough to be taken to the emperor himself. These leaders spent most of their day holding court in their provinces, hearing arguments and making decisions. They replicated the emperor's governing model, appointing advisory councils to gather information about the facts, opinions and climate of the province and advise them in rendering the many judgments their roles required. This advisory group usually consisted of experts in subjects the leader might need opinions on, such as finance, culture, and history.

Even though the existence of these advisory bodies became commonplace, their value became questionable. Some insightful people noticed something interesting happening in the courts. Few of the advisors ever challenged accepted wisdom, questioned status quo, or voiced concerns out of fear of displeasing their leader. The advisors frequently chose to keep their opinions, facts and perspectives to themselves ... when speaking up could have greatly influenced the leader's understanding of a given situation. Because of this, leaders ended up making faulty decisions due to the lack of awareness and understanding of all the variables involved. This system, while faulty, spread rapidly, eventually becoming tradition.

The attachment made me smile. I wondered who had written it. It certainly pointed out what could happen if a leader didn't have advisors who passed on truth, and it certainly applied as much today as it did back then. I often had thought that leadership, at its core, is a combination of awareness, understanding and action.

The catch, however, is that while many people are skilled and experienced in taking action, to be effective it must always be grounded in awareness and understanding. In a strange paradox, awareness and understanding are often sorely lacking in today's organizations. Because of this, many actions today's leaders choose miss the mark. Whether in the court in ancient China or in today's corporate boardrooms, leaders' decisions are only as good as the awareness and understanding on which they are based.

Whoever had written the attachment had certainly figured out a core leadership challenge. To take positive action, leaders desperately need access to awareness and understanding. They need to know the reality, the unedited truth, about themselves and their organizations: truth regarding how they are perceived, truth regarding the variables connected to any particular decision, truth regarding their organizational products and services, truth regarding the experience of their customers, and truth regarding the morale of the organization and the loyalty of their team. The list can go on and on.

The sad fact is that leaders often don't receive that truth. Leaders have often disconnected themselves (or become disconnected) from the ground-level, real-world happenings in their organizations, so they can't access the truth themselves. Far too often they respond by surrounding themselves with assistants, committees and advisors to provide them with the organizational truth they need access to. However, just like in ancient China, these advisors often become "yes men" (and "yes women") who end up mirroring the leader's own thoughts, fearful of disagreeing and assuming that supporting what they think is the management perspective is the best way for them to keep their job.

The end result is that leaders have blind spots in their awareness and understanding that keeps them from perceiving the whole picture.

I thought of a leadership team I was currently working with. They had absolutely no idea that the issue that was a major cause of the organization's lack of success was lack of customer service. It was common knowledge in the lower ranks of the company that customers perceived the company's service to be horrible: long telephone hold times, terrible return policies, pushy salespeople. That knowledge, as it made its way up the hierarchy, was watered down by those not wanting to pass on anything negative until the top leaders heard nothing at all. The leadership team not only lacked awareness and understanding of the true situation in their own company, but since they never heard anything negative they often asked their marketing department to laud their obviously good customer service on their consumer website. It was funny and a little sad.

I answered back:

Interesting! Times really haven't changed much! Leaders today face the same issues. The leaders I work with, more often than not, have a completely skewed perspective of themselves and their organizations. They continuously make decisions based on less than the whole story. They have blind spots that nobody helps them illuminate. The leadership issues they face usually stem directly from that circumstance!

I'm still a little fuzzy on the whole jester thing, though. How do jesters fit into all of this?

That's when a very curious thing happened. The moment I pressed Enter to send my e-mail, the reply to it appeared in my mailbox. How could that be? This was turning out to be fun.

Put aside the pictures that appear in your mind when you first think of jesters, but don't discard them completely quite yet. Everyone you ever talk to about jestership will start with those same perceptions. I'm going to replace them with others for you. You will have to replace them for those people. Read on ... we are getting close to the heart of the matter!

This e-mail also had an attachment. I opened it and grinned. Another scan, but this one looked like a copy of a restaurant menu! I could just make out the name of the place: The Cave's Diner. Someone had scribbled notes between the items on the menu and in the margins. I had to turn my head in different directions to read the whole text. The notes read:

The name of the first true jester may never be known, but it is a good assumption that at some point leaders in China realized the great risk they were taking surrounding themselves only with advisors who supplied no true advice, people who reflected only the leader's own opinions out of fear, ignorance, or self-preservation.

The need for a "teller of truth" became evident as these leaders realized they were taking action without awareness and understanding. During the time that this was becoming evident, something else was taking place. The traditional clowns that had entertained the court starting using their position to subtly comment more and more directly on the affairs of the day.

Since jesters often came to the court with no political status or aspirations and were not in a position to pose any kind of power threat to the leader, it became acceptable for jesters to completely speak their minds and for the leader to listen. In fact, they often did not feel the need to filter their words before speaking, which may account for the "foolishness" often ascribed to them.

Jesters, relying on the freedom from the restraints and fears of other advisors felt, were often able to express thoughts that no others would voice, thereby opening up new perspectives, insights, ideas and options to the leader. Because of this, in some courts, jesters' voices became more valued than those of the official advisors.

Often jesters were the only people to voice their opposition to ideas, and sometimes they were able to influence huge policy decisions. For instance, circa 300 B.C. the Chinese emperor Shih Huang-Ti was supervising the building of the famous Great Wall. As the wall neared completion, and although thousands of laborers died during its initial construction, Shi Huang-Ti was contemplating another phase: having the wall painted. If this project had been carried out it was predicted that many more Chinese laborers would lose their lives for what many saw as folly. Although Shih Huang-Ti had many advisors, his jester, Yu Sze, the official jester of the court, was the only one who openly criticized his plan. After laughing at the joking criticism, Shih Huang-Ti eventually decided to forgo the painting and ended the wall project. Today Yu Sze is credited with saving many lives and is celebrated as a national hero in China.

As more and more leaders learned to rely on their jesters' unique roles and abilities they noticed that, through them, they had increased access to insight and perspectives not previously accessible to them. They began to recognize truths that may have been at odds with their own perspectives and assumptions. Those who got past their own egos made better decisions. As a result, jesters became respected and valued in courts located far from where they began and could eventually be found at the side of leaders in China, Asia, and Europe.

Now, this caused me to sit back in my chair and think for a minute. This made sense. The concept of one person helping another challenge his own thinking sounded like what I had been trying to do for years. A jester was, by this definition, an advisor who challenged people to think in ways they themselves might not have considered. The jester perspective was intriguing. It provided a unique and fun way of looking at the relationship that could form between an advisee and advisor—a leader and a jester! Hmmm.

Another e-mail appeared as I was thinking:

You already ARE a jester. For years you have been struggling to do exactly what is at the core of jestership. It is time for you to step fully, consciously, into the role. The contribution you have been searching for is the contribution of a jester. Don't e-mail me back tonight. Just consider.

So I did. I spent the evening pondering the thoughts running through my mind. This felt right. Could I use the jester concept as a vehicle, as a perspective, to relay insights to leaders? As a jester, I could challenge these leaders to recognize their blind spots. In the same way those ancient jesters provided insights for emperors in ancient China, I could provide insights for leaders today! This could really change the way I contribute! I fell asleep that night with a smile on my face.

In the morning, another e-mail was waiting for me.

Your concept of "blind spots" is more insightful than you might imagine! They aren't just conceptual, they are real! People assume that what they perceive around themselves is what actually exists. For instance, take vision. Most understand what they "see" is only what their eye perceives and reports to their brain. The truth is much more complicated, and a lot stranger! In fact, your brain adds quite a bit to the report it gets from your eyes, so that a lot of what you think you see is actually made up by your brain! It doesn't exist. I want you to try something.

Close your left eye and stare at the X with your right eye from about a foot and a half away. Off to the right in your field of vision, you should be able to see the circle. Don't LOOK at the circle or change your focus, just notice that it is there. Now **slowly** *move your face towards the X. Keep staring directly at the X with your open eye while you move closer. At some point, the circle will disappear (it will reappear again if you move even closer). If it didn't seem to work the first time, try again, keeping focused on the X the whole time and moving your face closer to the X very slowly.*

```
┌─────────────────────────────────┐
│                                 │
│     X                      O    │
│                                 │
└─────────────────────────────────┘
```

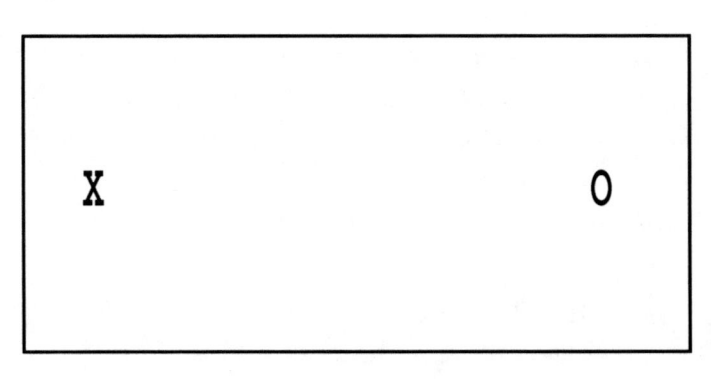

I tried it a couple of times. Nothing. Then I realized I wasn't really concentrating on the X, but staring out of the corner of my one open eye at the circle. I decided to give it one more try. As I slowly moved my head forward, the circle actually disappeared from my field of vision! I almost fell out of my chair!

Wow. What did you do to me?!?!

The answer came back in a flash.

Cool, isn't it? Each of our eyes has a region (where the optic nerve enters the eye) in which there are no visual receptors. When you moved your face towards the X you were adjusting your field of vision and, consequently, the place on your eye where the circle's image was hitting. When that image was positioned at exactly the right point (where the receptors couldn't perceive it), pop!, the circle disappeared!

Believe it or not, this happens to everyone, constantly, day in and day out! Most of the time we don't notice these blind spots because we are using both eyes (they cover for each other) and we are constantly sweeping our field of vision so objects don't stay in our blind spots for very long. Because of that, visual blind spots don't usually make much of an impact on our lives.

What's particularly interesting, though, is that in daily life we aren't even aware we **have** *these blind spots! In the experiment, when the spot disappeared from your field of vision you didn't notice a gaping hole, a black void or a big question mark. What you saw instead was a continuous white field where the circle was before. This is a lie that your brain is creating, since the eye isn't actually telling the brain anything at all about that particular part of your field of vision. Your brain simply "filled in" its best guess of what was probably there (in this case, a white area, since everything around the blind spot was white).*

Everyone has "blind spots" in aspects of their lives beyond the visual. They could exist as part of their leadership style, their perception of what is "true" in their organization, or their sense of how they relate to others. Often these kinds of blind spots are just as tricky to perceive as the visual one you discovered in the experiment. These blind spots do affect people's lives on a daily basis—especially the lives of those trying to influence organizations. People make decisions without all the information, continue behaviors that are destructive, and miss out on amazing opportunities … all because they exist within the blind spots. In fact, for most people, their brains are covering up for them, sending the message that they don't have blind spots at all!

So where are your blind spots? Want to find out?! Once jesters get good at discovering and addressing their own blind spots they can move on to helping other people discover theirs!

I sat back down in front of the computer and wrote back:

I get it. I see the wisdom of jesters. They uncover blind spots! It makes so much sense. I see blind spots around me all the time in the leaders I meet and the organizations I work with. I can use the perspective of a jester to help others uncover and address their own leadership blind spots! Now here is something for you!

I sent off a copy of a scanned article I had been keeping on my computer for years. I had found it fascinating since it addressed an interesting phenomenon I saw occurring in organizations all the time. I used to think the article pointed out lack of leadership. I now realized it was really pointing out absence of jestership! It showed just what would happen when a group didn't have insights into their blind spots. The article read:

A classic example of the misguided action that can occur when understanding is not present is exemplified in the Abilene Paradox. The paradox was illustrated by manage-

ment expert Jerry B. Harvey in his 1988 book *The Abilene Paradox and other Meditations on Management*. *Paraphrased, the story goes like this:*

One hot afternoon in Texas, four friends are playing a game on the porch of their house. One of them offhandedly suggests that they take a trip to Abilene, about an hour's drive away. The second member of the group agrees, saying, "Sounds like a great idea." Although the third member of the group is not particularly interested in the trip, he enthusiastically agrees, thinking that his real opinion is not in step with the rest of the group. The final member of the group, thinking that all the others have expressed a strong preference, says, "Of course I want to go. I haven't been to Abilene in a long time."

Seemingly in unanimous agreement, the four get into the car and leave. The drive ends up being warm, crowded, and long. When the group arrives back hours later, one of them dishonestly says, "It was a great trip, wasn't it?" The second member replies that she, actually, would rather have stayed home, but went along since the other three were so enthusiastic. The third member says, "I wasn't happy about going. I only went to go along with the rest of you." The final member says, "I just went along because you all wanted to go. I wasn't going to be the only one to say no. I thought you were all crazy to want to go out in this heat." Finally, the group member who offered the original idea admits that he only suggested it in the first place because he thought the others were bored!

The group sits back, perplexed that they decided, together, to take a trip that none of them actually wanted to take. They would have preferred to relax at the house but did not admit their own opinions when faced with the perception that they were in the minority. They spent the rest of the day thinking about what had happened and wondering whether it often occurred.

The response came back soon and was very short:

I have heard this story before, but what do you think it should mean to us?

I thought for a second and typed back:

I think that in organizations flawed actions result from an incomplete awareness and understanding of organizational truth. This lack of organizational truth happens because blind spots exist but aren't addressed—or even noticed! These unresolved blind spots result in choices and actions that are flawed, unfocused, or just plain inconsistent with what needs to be accomplished. Organizationally, blind spots cause inefficiencies ... loss of ROI (return on investment), lower morale, lost potential and, ultimately, lack of success.

As I was typing, I had another flash of insight:

Wait a minute. Something else just occurred to me! As a jester, I don't always have to feel a need to pass on specific solutions to issues. If I can help others see and address their own blind spots, they will start to recognize solutions to their own situations!

Wow. This was huge. I sent the message and almost immediately received a reply:

Now you are starting to get it. Jesters provide people access to truth by helping them recognize and address their own blind spots. Perform your role well and you will never have to sell any solution again. As people begin to recognize and eliminate blind spots, they will be able to perceive new information and insights, allowing them to create answers themselves. A much better way for people to learn! You will have passed on a tool they can use in the future rather than your one-time solution.

I thought for a moment and wrote back:

I am really starting to understand this concept, but does it work in the real world? Can companies tolerate jesters in the ranks? Can jesters make a difference?!

The next three e-mails came in one after another, all with the same subject line: Jesters in the real world. I opened the first one:

Ever hear of Southwest Airlines? That airline continues to be ranked in magazines such as Fortune *as one of the best companies to work for in America. How did they make it on the list? If you were to ask Southwest employees they will immediately point to Herb Keller. As the cofounder of Southwest Airlines, and its current chairman of the board, Keller has influenced the company in every possible way throughout the years.*

Southwest has always chosen its own path, often contrary to the standard, in virtually every area of airline operations. Because of this, Keller is well known within the company and the industry as a leader who has often gone against popular wisdom. Under Keller, Southwest started to offer low air fares that puzzled the competition, eliminated the airline meals that had been commonplace for years, stopped the traditional assigning of seats, encouraged flight attendants to spice up their in-flight emergency instructions, and became the first major airline to allow passengers to travel with electronic tickets.

All of these innovations were considered by many to be risky moves at the time. Keller didn't see it that way. He didn't bow to the advisors who told him the ideas went against tradition. He didn't worry about catering to the status quo. He didn't stop pushing his agenda when it seemed unpopular. What he did do was speak and act when he recognized something others didn't. Every time.

Throughout the years of Southwest's growth, Herb Keller proved again and again his ability to uncover opportunities when the competition couldn't or wouldn't. How did he do it? One of his secrets is his commitment to openness and honesty within his organization. He often encourages others to say what they think, even if it goes against the status quo, knowing that someone else may have an insight that others missed.

Since 1971, Southwest has also produced outstanding financial results, often during times when the other airlines were struggling. Keller's style, commitment, and unusual way of looking at leadership has produced not only a company that people love to work for, but also the tangible positive results that shareholders want.

In a 1994 article, Fortune *asked the question "Is Herb Keller America's Best CEO?" The subtitle of that article was very interesting and spoke to who Keller really is. It read: "Behind his clowning is a people-wise manager who wins when others can't."*

Keller is a jester.

I clicked on the second e-mail to open it:

While Keller is a great example of jestership in action, you certainly don't have to be on the board of directors at a Fortune 500 company to act as a jester might. Scott is a human resources team member at a large retail manufacturing company in Irvine, California. Although he is not in charge of the department, the influence he holds has expanded over the years. His colleagues view him as a valuable member of the team who often speaks his mind at meetings:

"Scott is always the one to point out alternatives to majority opinions, but he does it in a way that creates discussion and contemplation, not defensiveness. Around here he has the reputation of being the guy you go to when you want to know all the alternatives before you make a decision. He is great at coming up with perspectives, ideas or issues you hadn't considered before."

About a year ago, the Human Resources department was asked by the board of directors of the company to adjust the training that occurred within the company as part of a company-wide cost savings initiative. They were asked to dramatically reduce the amount of training hours per employee and slash the budget for training materials. Although many employees thought the decision was shortsighted, nobody dared challenge the decision because it came "from the top." Those who were asked their opinions hid their true thoughts and supported the decision, voicing their commitment to help the company in any way they could. Even those in the Human Resources department itself resigned themselves to carrying out the decree.

A couple of weeks after the announcement, the executive secretary got a call from Scott asking whether he could speak at the board of directors meeting scheduled later that week. Unheard of! Scott was granted his audience by a curious board. During the 10 minutes Scott was given to voice his thoughts, he said everything everyone else wished they could say: that training was important to the employees, that it affected morale and quality of work, that reducing training was penny wise but pound foolish. Scott brought stories from other companies and data from research to support his perspective. After 10 minutes the board members were stunned. They asked Scott why he was the only one passing on this information. Scott revealed that others weren't willing to tell the board their true thoughts out of fear of disagreeing with them and seeming unsupportive of the company's need to reduce costs. With that, the meeting adjourned.

Over the next couple of weeks the board was astounded when they uncovered the true feelings of their employees, and even more shocked to realize how much they had lost touch with the pulse of their organization.

In the end, not only did they end up reconsidering the training reduction, but they also resolved to better understand why people felt that they couldn't share their true opinions. As the weeks went on, and the discussions became more honest, long-held assumptions about the culture of the organization were tested. Later, Scott was recognized as the catalyst for discussions, realizations, and actions that would create a better and stronger company.

Scott is a jester.

By now I had started to grin. These were real people acting as jesters. I opened the third e-mail:

Jesters can exist not only in traditional corporations, but also in almost all organizations, even in the stereotypical structured universe of the scientific world. Richard Feynman was of those jesters. Most came to recognize him as a Nobel Prize-winning physicist but some knew his other side: an open-minded, curious man who loved to challenge the status quo. Richard Phillips Feynman was born in 1918 in Manhattan to parents who greatly influenced his view of life. Feynman's father encouraged his son's fascination with science, instilling a desire to question face values and dig deeper to find underlining themes. His dad taught him "the difference between knowing the name of something and knowing something," to quote one of Feynman's anecdotes.

Feynman reveled in the pleasure of exploring. He went to great lengths to model an image of a scientist that challenged the traditional stereotypes. He challenged his students to be dissatisfied with surface conclusions and to dig deeper for underlying answers. Since his childhood he had developed a habit of not taking anything for granted, of questioning everything, of pursuing whatever lay at the heart of any mystery.

As his stature as a scientist grew, so did his reputation for speaking his point of view without mincing words, no matter how much the audience might not want to hear his opinion. He often suspected that others couldn't see what he perceived and felt it was his responsibility to help them gain that perspective.

On January 28, 1986, the space shuttle "Challenger" exploded, killing all seven astronauts on board. A presidential commission was quickly appointed to study the tragedy and determine its cause. Feynman was asked to join it. He took his role very seriously and dove into all aspects of the study of the disaster. As he worked he noticed that he was asking questions others dared not ask. He started to be seen as a busybody, a person who didn't use the right channels, a troublemaker. After much hard work, Feynman eventually discovered the cause of the accident, but few believed his theory of an O-ring failure. Realizing that the people around him had blind spots that would not allow them to consider his theory, Feynman stopped trying to convince them; instead, he dramatically illustrated his theory at a televised committee meeting. He took a piece of O-ring rubber, dunked it in ice water, and showed the world that when it was cold it didn't return to its original shape quickly. The disaster's cause was uncovered. In hindsight, many question whether the committee would have discovered the cause of the incident without Feynman's continuous questioning of the surface conclusions they seemed satisfied with.

A colleague from the committee, General Donald Kutyna, said, "he brought this driving desire to get to the bottom of any mystery. No matter where it took him, he was going to get there, and he was not deterred by any roadblocks in the way. He was a courageous guy, and he wasn't afraid to say what he meant."

This is a way to summarize the way Feynman lived his life.

Feynman died in 1988, one of greatest physicists that the 20th century had produced. He was also a jester.

Wow! All of these people were acting in jestership and they may not have even known it. The paradigm of jestership does work in the real world ... it produced real results in real organizations! I wondered how common jesters were in the world ... or whether they could exist in all kinds of organizations. I spent that afternoon on the computer, searching various terms to uncover the faint tracks of jesters. Every so often, I saw the trail of a jester in a news story or organizational press release. It was amazing: **a secret world of extraordinary people making extraordinary impacts in their organizations.** I found the following:

- A regional sales manager for a very large, well-known national retail chain was being lauded by her employees for her ability to create a wonderful place to work. Her stores held the lowest turnover rate of any in the country and seemed to be filled with happy staff. I read that the employees attributed this success to her ability to be open to suggestions and opinions about her leadership as well as her willingness to speak up to management on behalf of her employees when nobody else would.
- A midlevel manager at a large national restau-

rant chain had just been moved into a unique position. Citing this woman's past ability to see and understand both the corporation's and restaurant owner's perspectives, she was asked to keep one foot in the frontline reality and the other in the management vision. Her job was to give a clear understanding of the viewpoints of each to those who only were able to perceive one or the other.

- A salesperson at a national consumer electronics chain was being recognized for her work throughout the year in creating innovation. She was lauded for ideas that she sent up the chain through her store to upper management. Some were implemented nationally. In the recognition speech it was noted that she had an ability to see things that others didn't, that she asked questions that others didn't think to ask, and that she spoke up in a way that got her ideas across but never seemed pushy.

In each of these people I saw elements of jestership. They had never heard of the term but were practicing aspects of it nevertheless. I realized that jestership could supply a structure, a model, for those special people who were already practicing aspects of it! There must be many out there. Some are probably struggling and don't have a name to label what they are trying to accomplish and who they are trying to be. They are jesters!

I wrote back:

I get it! Jestership can work! I can start using this new perspective tomorrow! I have been working with one particular leader for a couple of months. I'm going to adjust my coaching style. Instead of trying to pass on solutions to the leadership issues he is dealing with, we will start to focus on his blind spots. If he addresses those gaps he will see his own solutions to current issues as well as create a process to address future challenges! I clearly see his current blind spots; I'll just point them out to him! Is it really that simple?

The return e-mail came quickly:

Glad you are excited, but slow down a little. Like many other things in life, the concept is simple but the application is a bit tricky. Most people don't enjoy having their blind spots pointed out to them. Although true leaders have the profound ability to set aside their own egos and be completely open, they are a rare breed. People who have this ability often have gone beyond the need of jesters. Most of the people you meet in the world struggling with leadership aren't even close. Their egos get in the way. Remember, not only are they probably unaware of their own blind spots, but their brains may have found a way to cover them up. You could be entering a minefield of denial, defensiveness, or plain rejection.

To join the ranks of jesters you have to recognize they have traditionally played roles in very delicate relationships. His-

torically, while some people completely understood the value a jester's perspective brought them, many others had huge egos and short tempers and barely tolerated any of their advisors, especially those who might have wanted to talk about something like blind spots.

In those cases, jesters had to figure out how to deliver information in a way that would not bruise egos or incur wrath. Many jesters lost their lives if they couldn't figure out how to perform this feat. You may not lose your life these days, but you will certainly lose colleagues, clients, or friends if you can't master this skill!

I thought about all the people I had worked with over the years and realized my mysterious new pen pal was right. The variety of attitudes about self-improvement was incredibly diverse. Some people were ready and willing to hear other perspectives or feedback about themselves. These people wanted to learn, to be challenged. Others were much more resistant to anything that sounded like criticism. They would resist, stubbornly clinging to their entrenched world-views, disregarding anyone who was bold enough to suggest they had blind spots.

I typed back:

You are right. Sad, but true. Many people—most people—aren't ready to be directly confronted with their own blind spots.

I felt a little down about what I had written until I received the following in return:

*You said something profound. Most people don't want to be **directly** confronted with their blind spots. The true skill of a jester lies not only in being able to recognize blind spots, but also in understanding how to assist others to become aware of them, without bruising egos.*

A true jester is tricky, intelligent, and creative and has learned techniques to nudge people toward recognizing their blind spots without seeming confrontational. It's a little like suggesting that people move their faces toward the X in the experiment we did. Historically, clever jesters learned to deliver blind spot information, insights, and advice embedded in stories, myths, and legends they told in court. In that way, they avoided the risks inherent in giving leaders direct advice and skillfully nudged them toward discovering something themselves. Often, after hearing jesters speak, leaders believed they alone had teased out something profound. The jester knew differently.

Now, that sounded like fun! People could leave interactions with jesters with something useful, recognition of a blind spot that was keeping them from recognizing their own leadership solutions. The best part is that they would also never feel overly challenged or defensive about the process that brought the awareness about! Wonderful!

The next e-mail exchange came fast and furious:

I like the idea! So how do I start?!

I waited for the response:

Practice is really at the core of jestership. Eventually, you will not only be able to recognize blind spots but also to recognize the best way to guide others toward perceiving their own. The ability to choose just the right method to reveal blind spots is something you will get better at over time. Starting out you may need a little help. The very first step is to start training your mind to think *like a jester's! You will be receiving a package in a couple of days. Enjoy it!*

A package? This was going to move past e-mails! I asked:

What package? And how do you know my address?

The response was a bit vague:

Wait and see. Enjoy the suspense ... and the fun!

The next days were difficult. Every e-mail I sent went unanswered. Finally, four days later, a package arrived. It was small and square, delicately wrapped with no return address. I opened the brown wrapper and deftly caught a notecard that fell out of the packaging. It read:

> *A gift from one jester to another. Use this to*

sharpen your thinking. Apply what you discover inside to tease out your own blind spots, and soon you will be able to help others to do the same.

Within the wrapping was a small leather-bound book. It looked old. The embossed title on the front cover read, in flowing text, **Apprentice Jestership: Training Your Mind.** I laughed, opened the book to the introduction, and started reading:

Welcome! You are holding this book because someone has recognized your potential as a jester. At some point in the future you are going to dazzle those around you with your insights and your ability to pass those insights on to others clearly, subtly and enjoyably. Until you are able to accomplish that on your own, this book can assist you in training your mind to think like a jester's.

On the following pages, you will find stories that have been used for centuries by jesters to uncover blind spots surrounding a variety of organizational issues. These stories, while entertaining in themselves, can be used to prompt some hard questions ... probing areas people may not have ever thought about before.

This is the essence of jestership: the ability to access truth lying hidden and undiscovered in the blind spots. In probing for these truths, you will also uncover actions that can be taken to address real-world situations.

Actively pursuing the trains of thought the stories provide will allow you to access a more complete understanding of yourself and others, which can reveal opportunities for marvelous focused action.

Potential areas where blind spots may lurk will be presented through stories, metaphors and mythology. Each tale will be followed by some classic interpretations, thoughts and actions that have been used as follow-up to the stories throughout the years.

Be sure to try to figure out what kind of blind spot each story is illuminating before you turn the page. Although some questions are asked at the organizational level, each can be easily applied to a department or a team. Feel free to interpret the questions at the level at which you have influence and accountability in your particular situation.

Start by reading the stories and thinking how each may apply to you personally, then think about who else could benefit from thinking about them. Remember: try to glean meaning from the stories yourself, before you move on to the thoughts for you to ponder and actions a jester might consider taking. You may notice that many of the actions involve others. Blind spots cannot be completely uncovered or addressed alone. To really illuminate them, to reduce them, you will need the participation of others. Some of the actions recommended will require this. Good luck, and enjoy yourself!

Snow White, Mirror Measurement, and Self-Delusion

Once upon a time in midwinter, when the snowflakes were falling like feathers from heaven, a beautiful queen sat sewing at her window, which had a frame of black ebony. As she sewed, she looked up at the snow and pricked her finger with her needle. Three drops of blood fell into the snow. The red on the white looked so beautiful that she thought, "If only I had a child as white as snow, as red as blood, and as black as this frame." Soon afterward she had a little daughter who was as white as snow, as red as blood, and as black as ebony, and therefore they called her Little Snow White.

Now the queen was the most beautiful woman in all the land, and very proud of her beauty. She had a mirror, which she stood in front of every morning, and asked, "Mirror, mirror, on the wall, who in this land is fairest of all?" And the mirror always replied, "You, my queen, are fairest of all." Only then did she know for certain that no one in the world was more beautiful than she.

Now, Snow White grew up, and when she was seven years old she was so beautiful that she surpassed even the queen herself. Now when the queen asked her mirror who in the land was fairest of all the mirror answered, "You, my queen, are fair; it is true. But Little Snow White is a thousand times fairer than you."

Instead of smashing the mirror, the queen devised a sinister plot to kill Snow White to regain her status. After the plan had been carried out the queen was happy, went home, and asked the mirror her usual question. The mirror answered, "You, my queen, are fairest of all."

The queen's anger and actions had not gone unnoticed by the mirror. The answer to the queen's question would forever more be the same, no matter what the reality.

Uncover blind spots in how you are perceived as a leader.

Questions a Jester Might Ponder

- What method do you use to receive feedback on your leadership? How often do you consult this "mirror"? What do you do with the feedback?
- How do you know that your mirror is accurate? How do you know it is not just giving you what you want to hear?
- Who do you hold as a model for exceptional leadership? What are you doing to close the gap between your behavior and theirs?

Actions a Jester Might Consider Taking

- Create a new mirror for yourself by establishing an ongoing feedback mechanism for others to express how they perceive you as a leader. It must provide you with leadership feedback that is specific, timely, and actionable. A "360-degree" feedback tool would be perfect.
- Make a personal commitment to be more open to feedback and to act on any you receive. Take one action per week that reflects this commitment.
- Publicly show your openness to receiving feedback. Comment about your willingness to receive it in a memo, the company newsletter, etc. Be honest and never punish someone for taking you up on the offer.

Communication, Understanding, and an Ancient Stone

Until the deciphering of hieroglyphics, not much was known about the ancient Egyptians. Although the civilization had been mentioned in the Bible, historians didn't know much about it since the code to their written language had not been discovered. The life of early Egyptians continued to be shrouded in mystery until one summer in the late 1700s when a fortuitous event occurred. A group of soldiers stumbled across a stone tablet covered with strange markings, near the city of Rosetta in Egypt.

This tablet, later called the "Rosetta Stone," was handed over to French scientists, who declared that something of incredible value had been found. Although some of the writing on the stone was ancient Greek, much of the text on the stone was in hieroglyphics. After some study, it was concluded that the Greek text was written by a group of priests in Egypt to honor the pharaoh. As the scientists continued to examine the stone, they realized the same text was repeated not only in ancient Greek but also in two forms of Egyptian hieroglyphics! It was thought to have been originally written in three scripts so that the priests, government officials, and rulers of Egypt (who all used different languages in their daily life) could all read what it said.

After many years of study, a French scholar named Jean Champollion was able to use his knowledge of the Greek text to translate the Egyptian writing. Following Champollion's breakthrough, it became possible to understand other hieroglyphic texts, and many of the mysteries of ancient Egyptian civilization were unlocked. To this day, our broad knowledge of Egyptian life can be traced back to the unearthing and translation of the Rosetta Stone.

Uncover blind spots in your ability to communicate with others.

Questions a Jester Might Ponder

- Which of your daily interactions has the most risk of being misunderstood? Why?
- What technical terms, specific language, or internal acronyms do you use that others (colleagues, customers, vendors, etc.) may not be able to translate or understand? Are you making assumptions about what people know?
- How is your communication style different from the style of those you communicate with? Do you adjust when appropriate to make sure your message is received and understood?

Actions a Jester Might Consider Taking

- What communication methods (e-mail, telephone, voice mail, blackberry, in-person communication sessions, executive blogs, Q&A sessions, internal speeches, etc.) does the organization use? Should it adopt some it is not using? Which are most prone to being misunderstood? Why?
- Make a list of the terms/acronyms/phrases that are used in the organization that might not be fully understood (by new members, clients, etc.) Create a dictionary (paper or online) of the terms and their meanings.

- Use a communication assessment tool to understand your style and language and how they may differ from those of people around you.
- Create "Rosetta Stone" meetings with the colleagues you work most closely with. These gatherings have the sole purpose of making sure everyone clearly shares the same understanding of any information currently in the organization that pertains to the group.

Note:

Feel free to continue reading the Apprentice Guide stories or skip to page 83 if you want to see what happens after Dave reads the guide. You can return to read the stories later in any order. You may even find yourself returning to the individual stories many times to find new insights.

Promotion, Hesitation, and the Sword of Damocles

There once was a king named Dionysius. He lived in a fine palace with beautiful and costly things, and he was waited upon by a host of servants who were always ready to do his bidding.

Naturally, because Dionysius had so much wealth and power, there were many in the city who envied his good fortune. Damocles was one of these. He could often be heard saying, "How lucky you are Dionysius! You have everything anyone could wish for. You must be the happiest man in the world."

One day Dionysius grew tired of hearing such talk. "Do you really think I'm happier than everyone else?" "But of course you are," Damocles replied. "Look at the great treasures you possess, and the power you hold. You have not a single worry in the world. How could life be any better?"

"Perhaps you would like to change places with me," said Dionysius.

"Oh, I would never dream of that," said Damocles. "But if I could only have your riches and your pleasures for one day, I should never want any greater happiness."

"Very well. Trade places with me, and you shall have them."

And so, the next day, Damocles was led to the palace, and all the servants were instructed to treat him as their master. They dressed him in royal robes, and placed on his head a crown of gold. He sat down at a table in the banquet hall, and rich foods were set before him. Nothing was wanting that could give him pleasure. There were costly wines, and beautiful flowers, and rare perfumes, and delightful music. He rested himself among soft cushions, and felt he was the happiest man in all the world.

"Ah, this is the life," he sighed to Dionysius, who sat at the other end of the long table. "I've never enjoyed myself so much."   And as he raised a cup to his lips, he lifted his eyes toward the ceiling. What was that dangling above him, with its point almost touching his head? Damocles stiffened. The smile faded from his lips, and his face turned ashy pale. His hands trembled. He wanted no more food, no more wine, no more music. He only wanted to be out of the palace, far away, he cared not where. For directly above his head hung a sword, held to the ceiling by only a single horsehair. Its sharp blade glittered as it pointed right between his eyes. He started to jump up and run, but stopped himself, frightened that any sudden move might snap the thin thread and bring the sword down. He sat frozen in his chair.

"What is the matter, my friend?" Dionysius asked. "You seem to have lost your appetite."

"That sword! That sword!" whispered Damocles. "Don't you see it?"

"Of course I see it," said Dionysius. "I see it every day. It always hangs over my head, and there is always the chance someone or something may cut the slim thread. Perhaps one of my own advisors will grow jealous of my power and try to kill me. Or someone may spread lies about me, to turn people against me. It may be that a neighboring kingdom will send an army to seize this throne. Or I might make an unwise decision that will bring my downfall. If you want to be a leader, you must be willing to accept these risks. They come with the power, you see."

"Yes, I do see," said Damocles. "I see now that I was mistaken, and that you have much to think about besides your riches and fame. Please take your place, and let me go back to my own house."

And as long as he lived, Damocles never again wanted to change places, even for a moment, with the king.

Uncover blind spots in your understanding of the situation and pressures of those around you in the organization.

Questions a Jester Might Ponder

- What are the current swords of Damocles (goals, deadlines, pressures) felt by those around you? Which of those can you influence?
- What swords do you feel are hanging over your head? Is it possible that any of them are erroneous self-perceptions?
- Has fear of your swords affected your behavior?
- What can you do to lessen the fear of the swords for yourself and those around you?

Actions a Jester Might Consider Taking

- Take time to analyze the threads holding your swords. Which ones are truly fraying and which are much stronger than you might think?
- Discuss the swords that are consistently hanging over your head with the appropriate members of your organization. Each week commit to ease the fear of at least one sword for another person.
- Encourage others to be more open in revealing their swords to the organization so that others may assist them.

Lost History, Atlantis, and Reinventing the Wheel

Once, long ago, the gods of old divided the land so that each god might own a lot. Poseidon, god of the sea, was bequeathed a beautiful island that he called Atlantis.

The inhabitants of the island were considered far and wide to be a noble and powerful race. Thanks to the natural resources found throughout their island the people who lived their lives there had few wants or needs. Poseidon influenced the weather so that two harvests were possible each year, one in the winter fed by the rains and one in the summer fed by irrigation from the canal.

Besides the harvests, the island provided all kinds of herbs, fruits, and nuts. An abundance of animals, including elephants, roamed the island. Due to the easy life they had, Atlanteans had the time and energy to devote to many other things. They began to make huge advances in technology, culture, and philosophy.

For generations the Atlanteans lived simple, virtuous lives. But slowly they began to change. They started to take for granted the easy life they had on the island and the things they had been given. Greed and power began to corrupt them. Harvests began to be disregarded and fruit and vegetable died on the vines. When Zeus saw the immorality of the Atlanteans he gathered the other gods to determine a suitable punishment. They decreed that the era of Atlantis should come to an end. Zeus commanded Poseidon to call up the seas in a violent surge. The water crashed into the island, sweeping from one end to the other. When the waves subsided, the island of Atlantis, its people, and its memory had been swallowed by the sea. Nothing was left. Future civilizations had lost the knowledge that Atlantis had accumulated and had to start all over again.

Uncover blind spots in your ability to understand and leverage organizational history.

Questions a Jester Might Ponder

- Is your organization taking for granted the history that created the present?
- Do you have any gaps in your understanding of your organization's history?
- What mistakes have been made in the past that should not be repeated? Do you know enough about past circumstances to ensure they won't occur again?
- What organizational history is at risk of being lost because it was not, or is not, being documented?
- Where in the organization is the wheel being reinvented because past history is not being considered?

Actions a Jester Might Consider Taking

- Take time to talk to people that have been at the organization longer than you. Make it your intention to find out the history of your department, what mistakes have been made in the past and how were they resolved, and what accomplishments have been critical in the organization's history.
- Start a process to document history in your department. Talk to staff in the human resources

department to begin a milestone program to capture and enshrine significant events and accomplishments.
- Think about your contributions to the organization. What will be remembered in the organizational history in one year? Five years? Ten years? How can you make sure the history is written the way you prefer it to be?

The Olympic Flame and Personal Branding

In ancient Greece fire was an important sign. It symbolized the creation of the world, renewal, and light. It was also the sacred symbol of Hephaestus, and a gift to the human race from Prometheus, who stole it from Zeus. At the center of every city-state in ancient Greece there was an altar with an ever-burning fire, and in every home the sacred flame burned, dedicated to Hestia, goddess of the family.

Torch relay races started in ancient Greece as religious rituals held at night. Soon they turned into a team athletic event, initially among adolescents, and further developed to become one of the most popular ancient sports. The enchanting power of fire was a source of inspiration. Sacred flames lit by the rays of the sun always burned in Olympia, in an altar dedicated to Hestia. Fire was ignited with the help of a concave mirror, which has the ability to concentrate the rays of the sun on a single spot. When the head priestess touched that point with the torch, the flame was lit.

The ancient Greeks held a *lampadedromia* (the Greek word for torch relay), in which athletes competed by passing on the flame in a relay race to the finish line. In ancient Athens the ritual was performed during the *Panathenaia* festival, held every four years in honor of the goddess Athena. The strength and purity of the sacred flame was preserved through its transportation by the quickest means, in this case a relay of torchbearers. The torch relay runners carried the flame from the altar of Prometheus to the altar of Athena on the Acropolis. Forty youths from the 10 Athenian tribes had to run a distance of 2.5 kilometers in total. No matter where they ran, day or night, the flame could be seen. The torch became the outward symbol of what the torchbearer believed in and was committed to. By carrying it openly and proudly, there was no confusion as to the values and priorities of the bearer.

Uncover blind spots in your organizational branding.

Questions a Jester Might Ponder

- How are you branded within your organization? Is it clear what torches you carry? To yourself? To your colleagues? To your staff? To your supervisor?
- Have your torches changed throughout the years? Which have grown dimmer or gone out? Which have brightened? Why?
- What torches does your organization want you to be carrying? Is it obvious to others through your words and actions that you are bearing them?

Actions a Jester Might Consider Taking

- Make a list of the expressed priorities of your organization. Then, create a matching list of daily activities and behaviors that would reflect those priorities.
- Decide who has the best "branding" in your organization. Schedule some time with him or her to discuss this perception.
- Plan specific ways to display your torches more openly and obviously in your actions.

Icarus, Overconfidence, and Organizational Insight

A long time in the past, Daedalus and his son Icarus were imprisoned in Crete by Minos for insulting a relation of this great king. Father and son spent night after night plotting an escape from the prison, discarding plan after plan as impractical. Daedalus, who was known throughout the land as a great inventor, pondered night after night a fantastic invention that might assist them. Finally, he stumbled on a very clever idea. To escape from the seemingly inescapable prison, Daedalus decided to make wings of feathers and wax for himself and his son and fly out of the prison as birds! He began to construct the wings, using all of his renowned skill and knowledge. The final wings were well designed, very strong, and cleverly built.

Daedalus, examining the wings, had great faith in his construction but also understood the danger of overconfidence, so he warned his son to fly neither too low nor too high when they escaped. Too low, he explained, and the wings would be ruined by water from the sea and too high and the sun might melt the wax holding the delicate pieces of the wings together. The day finally came and father and son donned their wings. They jumped from a high tower and smiled as the wings held them both aloft. As both flew beyond the prison walls, climbing into the clouds, onlookers below stared upward, not believing what they saw. The crowds of people below pointed, shouted, and gawked.

As they glided away Icarus looked down at the people and realized that he held their attention. He thought he might impress them by flying even higher. As Icarus continued to climb he forgot his father's advice and grew careless, flying closer and closer to the sun. As he flew higher the heat continued to rise until the wax in the wings melted and the wings fell apart around him. Icarus quickly fell to earth and plunged into the sea. Daeldalus looked for his son's body to wash up on land but eventually only recovered a few feathers.

He was never to see Icarus again.

Uncover blind spots in your awareness of risk in the organization.

Questions a Jester Might Ponder

- What are the true "wings" of your role, department, and organization? What characteristics, situations, or processes have allowed you to be successful to date that cannot be put at risk?
- What three specific current organizational behaviors, projects, or policies are putting your "wings" at risk? What can you do to mitigate the risks?
- Where do you feel overconfidence exists in the organization? Why? How can you share your concerns?

Actions a Jester Might Consider Taking

- Establish a ongoing risk assessment meeting to discuss "wings" that may be at risk.
- Have a conversation with your supervisor, mentor, or close colleague. Ask him or her to share where he or she sees you being overconfident.
- Make a conscious decision about how much risk you are willing to take on in your work.

The Cat, the Fox, and Commitment to Lifelong Learning

It happened that a cat met Mr. Fox in the woods. She thought, "He is intelligent and well experienced, and is highly regarded in the world," so she spoke to him in a friendly manner: "Good-day, my dear Mr. Fox. How is it going? How are you? How are you getting by in these hard times?"

The fox, filled with arrogance, examined the cat from head to feet, and for a long time did not know whether he should give an answer. At last he said, "Oh, you poor beard-licker, you speckled fool, you hungry mouse hunter, what are you thinking? Have you the nerve to ask how I am doing? What do you know? How many tricks do you understand?"

"I understand but one," answered the cat, modestly.

"What kind of a trick is it?" asked the fox.

"When the dogs are chasing me, I can jump into a tree and save myself. Shall I teach you how?"

"Is that all?" said the fox. "I am master of a hundred tricks, and I have been around much, much longer than you. My tricks have always worked for me and I have no need to learn more."

Just then a hunter came by with four dogs ... a very new way to hunt. The cat jumped nimbly up a tree and sat down at its top, where the branches and foliage completely hid her.

"Quickly use one of your many tricks," the cat shouted to him, but four dogs were too many for the fox.

"Oh, Mr. Fox," shouted the cat. "You and your hundred tricks are left in the lurch. If you had wanted to learn just one more you would not have lost your life."

Uncover blind spots in your ability to keep up with the times.

Questions a Jester Might Ponder

- Where in your organization is there too much reliance on the status quo? In your own knowledge and actions? How are you and your organization falling behind because of it?
- How many hours a week do you spend in dedicated learning or training? What would be the pros and cons of doubling that number?
- How are you personally learning from new members entering the organization?
- How fast is your organizational marketplace or customer base changing? What specific things is your organization doing to keep its members current?

Actions a Jester Might Consider Taking

- Commit a certain period of time each week to learning. Mark it out on your calendar. Read an industry magazine, attend a training class, or use the Internet for research.
- Make a conscious decision to learn two new things every week: one piece of knowledge and one skill.
- Determine what areas of your organization are

becoming stagnant and devise a plan to encourage learning in that area.
- Join a professional organization that provides networking opportunities. Use the network to discover "things that you don't know that you don't know."

Statements of Mission, Blind Men, and an Elephant

It was six men of Indostan
> To learning much inclined,
Who went to see the Elephant
> (Though all of them were blind)
That each by observation
> Might satisfy his mind.

The First approached the Elephant,
> And happening to fall
Against his broad and sturdy side,
> At once began to bawl:
"God bless me! but the Elephant
> Is very like a wall!"

The Second, feeling of the tusk,
> Cried, "Ho! what have we here
So very round and smooth and sharp?
> To me 'tis mighty clear
This wonder of an Elephant
> Is very like a spear!"

The Third approached the animal,
> And happening to take
The squirming trunk within his hands,
> Thus boldly up he spake:
"I see," quoth he, "the Elephant
> Is very like a snake!"

The Fourth reached out an eager hand,
    And felt about the knee.
"What most this wondrous beast is like
    Is mighty plain," quoth he;
"'Tis clear enough the Elephant
    Is very like a tree!"

The Fifth, who chanced to touch the ear,
    Said: "E'en the blindest man
Can tell what this resembles most;
    Deny the fact who can
This marvel of an Elephant
    Is very like a fan!"

The Sixth no sooner had begun
    About the beast to grope,
Than, seizing on the swinging tail
    That fell within his scope,
"I see," quoth he, "the Elephant
    Is very like a rope!"

And so these men of Indostan
    Disputed loud and long,
Each in his own opinion
    Exceeding stiff and strong,
Though each was partly in the right,
    And all were in the wrong!

. . .

John Godfrey Saxe

Uncover blind spots in your organization's statement of mission.

Questions a Jester Might Ponder

- Does your company have a mission statement? If not, why not? If so, what percentage of the organization could recite it?
- How is your organization's mission stated? How many ways can it be interpreted? Is the wording specific and behavior-oriented?
- Is your organizational mission understood and applicable at the department level? The individual level? Is it specific enough to guide behavior?
- How have you clarified the mission of the organization for those you lead? Do they perceive the whole elephant or individual parts?

Actions a Jester Might Consider Taking

- Take the overall organizational mission statement and rewrite it for your department or area. Your new statement should be specific to your department, be rooted in behaviors, and clearly uphold the organizational mission.
- Determine how your mission statement should be modeled in actual daily *behaviors*. Discuss those behaviors for each person you lead and, after agreement, hold them accountable for displaying them.

Leader Identification, Hidden Talent, and the Sword in the Stone

During the age of dragons, wizards, and magic, few tales were as well known as the exploits of King Arthur. Before this age of Camelot, however, Arthur, the true heir to the throne of Uther Pendragon, was unknown to the kingdom. His heritage had been lost in a plot by evil forces that had their eyes on the throne. Evil men conspired to kidnap Arthur as a baby to ensure that he never would reach manhood. To save Arthur from this plot it was decided that he should be hidden from those who were seeking him before they had a chance to steal him away. So, as a tiny baby, Arthur was taken from his true parents by Merlin the wizard and raised as a commoner by another couple. This successfully hid his true heritage as Arthur grew up. No one in the kingdom suspected Arthur was the true heir to the throne, including Arthur himself!

After the death of Uther, the barons of the kingdom were faced with identifying a successor. This was controversial and hotly contested. The infighting eventually caused them to turn to Merlin for counsel. Merlin, knowing the true situation, asked the barons to approve a magical test to determine the true heir. After working on the task, Merlin invited the barons to a cathedral where they found a sword buried in an anvil. Merlin explained the seemingly simple test: only the true king would be able to remove the sword.

During the weeks and months that followed many visited the kingdom to try to remove the great sword, but all failed. Crowds assembled each day as royalty from distant lands came to try their luck. Each failed. One day, however, Arthur decided to try, to the amusement of the crowd. He grabbed the sword with this right hand and easily slipped the sword from the anvil. The crowd went silent, astonished. Arthur, surprised himself, repeated removing the sword a number of times for the barons who were quickly called. The barons eventually recognized Authur for who he was and crowned him king. Thus began the reign of Arthur and the golden age of Camelot.

Uncover blind spots in the way your organization leverages potential.

Questions a Jester Might Ponder
- How does your organization define people with "high potential"?
- How does your organization currently identify those with high potential? Is this process consistent, fair, and far-reaching?
- Which areas of your organization (departments, locations, roles) are being excluded from the search? Why? What risks are you facing because of this?
- When someone with high potential is identified, what is done to ensure she or he reaches that potential?
- How does your organization ensure diversity? Is the result diverse enough to ensure you don't miss a chance to recruit or retain an Arthur?

Actions a Jester Might Consider Taking
- Create an ongoing "sword in the stone" test to identify those in your organization with untapped ability. It could be a monthly challenge, a volunteer opportunity, or ongoing management accountability.

- Create a program to develop high potentials once they are identified. This could be anything from a formalized program to a personal mentorship.

The Spoken Word, the Gutenberg Bible, and Organizational Communication

For generations of human history knowledge was passed using stories and legends told by elders to the young. History, skill, technological advances—everything, in fact—was transferred orally. If important thoughts did not get enshrined into tales told and retold, that knowledge was lost. This continued until a new technology affected the way information could be transferred.

When books appeared on the scene, everything changed. Thoughts could now be captured and passed on to people without memorizing a story. The transfer of thoughts was not limited by geography, language, or even time! The first texts were individually hand-written on scrolls. These works of art were carefully crafted by monks and could take months or even years to finish. These first books were, by definition, one of a kind. Because of their rarity, initially books were not widely read. Even though the invention of books had huge potential, most general knowledge continued to be passed by individual to individual and generation to generation via the spoken word. Something else had to happen.

In the early 1400s a man named Johann Gutenberg began to experiment with printing techniques. After having some success with new methods, Gutenberg set up a press and tried to print books. He began by printing large Latin Bibles and using his hand-set type casts to print multiple copies. This innovation profoundly affected the availability of books, since multiple copies of the same text could be easily and efficiently made. Gutenberg's invention created a new way to spread knowledge throughout Europe without relying on the spoken word and eventually helped the Renaissance come about. His invention had a momentous effect on the average person's access to ideas and information. Unknowingly, Gutenberg forever changed the way human beings communicate with each other that has lasted to this day.

Uncover blind spots in the way information flows in your organization.

Questions a Jester Might Ponder

- How is critical information being spread throughout your organization? Is that method more similar to the spoken word or to the Gutenberg press? How would members of your organization rate the quality of internal communication?
- Does information flow both up and down the hierarchy of your organization? How would you assess the quality of flow in both directions?
- What critical information flows through the organization? What doesn't? Why not?
- Who decides what information is passed on to the organization?

Actions a Jester Might Consider Taking

- Discuss with your colleagues how information flows through your organization. Take an honest look at the gaps.
- Create a "Gutenberg press" (an internal newsletter, website, or bulletin board) for your organization that ensures that critical, consistent, organized information flows to everyone. The "press" should be consistent, ongoing, and timely. It should also allow for involvement and

feedback from organizational members at all levels.
- Develop opportunities for rich, two-way communications between management and employees (lunch and learn sessions, coffee talks, small focus groups, etc.).

The Old Man, Personal Ethics, and the Scorpion

One morning, after he had finished his meditation, an old man opened his eyes and saw a scorpion floating helplessly in the water.

As he watched, the scorpion was washed closer to a tree. The old man quickly got up, stretched himself out on one of the long roots that branched out into the river, and reached out to rescue the drowning creature.

As soon as he touched it, the scorpion stung him. Instinctively, the man withdrew his hand. A minute later, after he had regained his balance, he stretched himself out again on the roots to save the scorpion. This time the scorpion stung him so badly with its poisonous tail that his hand became swollen and bloody and his face contorted with pain.

Again, after a moment, the man reached for the scorpion. At that moment, a passerby saw the old man stretched out on the roots struggling with the scorpion and shouted, "Hey, stupid old man, what's wrong with you? Only a fool would risk his life for the sake of an ugly, evil creature. Don't you know you could kill yourself trying to save that ungrateful scorpion?"

The old man turned his head. Looking into the stranger's eyes he said calmly, "My friend, just because it is the scorpion's nature to sting, that does not change my nature to save."

Uncover blind spots in the congruence between values and behaviors.

Questions a Jester Might Ponder

- Which of the following do you see as your core personal values?:
Honesty, Kindness, Respectfulness, Integrity, Truthfulness, Courage, Power, Responsibility, Loyalty, Duty, Persistence, Empathy, Forgiveness, Understanding, Tolerance, Humility, Right Attitude, Openness, Harmony, Prestige, Cooperation, Dependability. Note: these particular values are subjective. Feel free to add to the list.
- Think of a time when you behaved in a way that wasn't in line with your stated core values. Why did you choose to violate them? Would you again?
- What current organizational practices are not in line with your stated values? What are you going to do about that incongruence?

Actions a Jester Might Consider Taking

- Spend some time defining your personal ethics. Write down the core values that are non-negotiable. How are these expressed in your daily behaviors?
- Give colleagues the above value list and ask them to tell you what they think your three most

important core values are. See whether their perceptions match yours.
- Share the list with your colleagues. Explain which of the values are most important to you and why they are so essential. Discuss whether they share the same values.

Hercules, Hero Creation, and Organizational Training

The day before Hercules was born Zeus proclaimed that his son would rule the house of Perseus, at the time the most revered family line.

After the boy was born, Zeus tried to make good on his boast by enlisting the greatest minds of the age in training Hercules in all the skills he would need to become a true hero. Among his teachers was Amphitryon, who taught him chariot driving; Castor, who passed on the art of fencing; Cheiron, a centaur, who helped Hercules understand the meaning and value of manners and decorum; and Linus, who introduced him to literature. After this kind of attention it was no surprise that Hercules was delivered back to Zeus ready to take on the mantle of hero.

During his adolescence, Hercules found himself embroiled in a long-standing battle between the Thebans and the Minyans. Since Thebes was his home, Hercules sided with the Thebans and eventually led an army that killed the king of the Minyans. After this battle, Hercules went temporarily mad, killing some of his own family members in his rage. After his sanity returned, Hercules traveled to Delphi to ask the oracle how he could atone for his deeds.

The oracle sent Hercules to Tiryns to perform 12 labors assigned to him by the king. These labors were immense tasks that had not been addressed for years. Some of the labors were perceived to be risky, some overwhelming, some distasteful. In completing these tasks, Hercules would not only atone for his crimes but would also be elevated to immortality and take his place among the gods. During the course of the labors, Hercules accomplished seemingly amazing feats, including the slaying of the hydra, the capturing of the hound of Hades, and the acquisition of the apples of Hesperides. Not all of the tasks were glamorous, however; he was also required to clean out the stables of Augeas, which housed over 5,000 head of cattle and had not been cleaned for over 30 years.

In the end, however, Hercules completed all the labors assigned to him and earned a place with the rest of the gods.

Uncover blind spots in the way work is perceived in your organization.

Questions a Jester Might Ponder

- Who are the heroes in your organization? Why are they perceived that way? How can one become a hero? What are the benefits of being seen as a hero?
- In each area of your organization identify the "labors": those necessary tasks that are perceived as risky, overwhelming, or distasteful. Are the people who accomplish the "labors" seen as heroes? Why or why not?
- How can you create more heroes in the organization? How can you better recognize those who are accomplishing the "labors"?

Actions a Jester Might Consider Taking

- Commit to a period of time each week to recognize contribution by others in your organization. Hand-sign notes of thanks, recognize them in newsletters or company-wide voice mails, etc.
- Create a system to officially recognize more people as "heroes" in your organization, especially those who accomplish the labors.

Corporate Vulnerability and the Weakness of Achilles

Thetis was a daughter of the sea god Nereus and had once been courted by Zeus. After his advances were spurned, Zeus became angry and decreed that Thetis could never marry another god. Thetis found and eventually learned to love the mortal Peleus, the King of Phythia, a city in Thessaly. Although she followed Zeus's wishes, she was not content to have a mere mortal as a son. Soon after Achilles was born Thetis researched the ways in which she could make him immortal. She had heard about the way in which Hercules' mortality had been burned off on a funeral pyre, which allowed his immortal part to ascend to Mount Olympus, and decided to try something similar while Achilles was still a baby. She traveled to the river Styx in Hades and dipped Achilles in. His mortality was indeed burned off and he became nearly immortal—except that the heel that Thetis held when she plunged him in had not been immersed.

As a youngster, Achilles was trained in the art of war and progressed very quickly, surpassing the expectations of his tutors and his father. It was even whispered that the Greeks could never end the Trojan War without his help.

Achilles, although still very young, was intrigued by the glory that could be his in the battle, and against his mother's wishes he joined the war as an admiral.

Before moving to attack Troy, the Greeks first raided the offshore island of Tenders. During the battle, Achilles killed King Tenes, a son of Apollo who valiantly tried to repel the invaders. Apollo was not at all pleased by this and would later return the favor by helping to kill Achilles.

During the many battles that followed, Achilles established himself as a great warrior who struck the decisive blow on many occasions. The war took a number of twists and turns, but eventually Achilles and the Greek army found themselves assaulting Troy itself. Inside the wall, Paris, the prince of Troy, found himself frantically letting arrow after arrow fly at the siege. Although Paris was not a very well regarded archer, Apollo chose that moment to intervene and guided one arrow unerringly, piercing the one place Achilles was vulnerable: his heel.

Uncover blind spots in the vulnerabilities in your organization.

Questions a Jester Might Ponder

- Describe the most vulnerable aspects of your organization or department, your processes, your products and/or services, your technology, your organizational structure, your manufacturing process, your customer base, your marketing plan, your five-year plan, etc. Do the same for your competition.
- How can you better shield the organizational Achilles' heels you have identified? How can you exploit the heels of your competition?
- Where do you feel personally vulnerable in your role?

Actions a Jester Might Consider Taking

- Make a list of the areas in which you personally feel vulnerable. Create a plan to slowly decrease your exposure.
- Organizationally, create a vulnerability list by department, task, or function. Start a task force to explore ways to take items off the list by internally partnering with each other.
- Create a plan to exploit a particular vulnerability you have uncovered in your competitor.

I finished the last page, closed the book, and smiled. They were simple, familiar stories, yet now I saw a new way to use them. In the role of jester, telling the stories provided a safe method of illuminating aspects of leadership. The stories created a dialog, a way to jumpstart a jester relationship with someone else. Discussion of the meaning behind the stories paved the way to probe for areas of blindness.

If I had had the stories to use as a tool with some of the people I had worked with in the past to focus in on their blind spots—and if they took on the new behaviors the stories suggested—they would have dramatically improved their ability to bring leadership to their organizations.

I pledged to read the stories over and over until I gleaned every last bit of personal application as I could. I planned to start that very evening. Later, as I lay in bed re-reading one of the stories, something seemed amiss.

I had another realization. Jestership, by its very nature, depended on human relationships. The very nature of blind spots made them very difficult to illuminate by oneself. Although the stories were interesting to read, and I did get some great self-reflection out of them, they wouldn't help me see anything but the faint traces of my own blind spots unless I involved other people. The stories provided a content that should be examined, discussed and pondered by people together. Sitting alone in an office or cubicle or den "thinking" about the stories wasn't going to produce much revelation. One had to "get out there," share the stories with others, enlist them into giving feedback, make them a part of the actions to consider. Jesters needed other jesters to develop themselves! Sometimes, I would play the jester for others, and sometimes someone else would be playing the jester for me! **Jestership is action-oriented and relationship-driven.**

I set the book down and I wandered over to the computer. I knew there would be a message waiting. Indeed, there was:

Dave, this will be my last e-mail for awhile. You have everything you need to continue on your journey. Continue to sharpen your mind to think like a jester. Become a jester for some. Help others become jesters themselves. Surround yourself with jesters and help each other develop. You will do just fine. As a little goodbye gift, the website is yours. Good luck. Make a difference.

I typed in "www.corporatejester.com" and saw that the "*Coming Soon*" banner had been replaced. It now read "*Better get to work, you have lots to share.*"

I laughed.

Over the weeks that followed, I worked on the website, trying to build a vehicle to pass on some of the insights I had gained from the e-mail exchange with my jester friend. I spent the evenings re-reading stories out of the handbook and thinking about how they illuminated blinds spots for me. I shared the stories with people I worked with and marveled at the insights we discovered about ourselves as we talked.

Over time, I came to realize the stories in the jester's handbook were only the beginning. Once you understand—really understand—true jestership, the quest to surround yourself with other jesters and to illuminate blind spots becomes a daily exercise. The secret recipe was not in the understanding or in the stories in the handbook, but in the commitment to jestership itself. That night I re-read all the e-mails and realized that they contained the real magic: the e-mail correspondence detailed my slow understanding of the true concept of jestership.

I continued to build the website into something that reflected my new understanding of jestership and leadership. Slowly, it took form, becoming a place for me to pass on what I had learned. It morphed into a place where I could offer my understanding of jestership to others and meet others who were jesters in their own part of the world.

One evening, as I typed an e-mail to someone who had visited the site and wanted to hear more, I realized that there were other ways to pass on what I had experienced. How about writing it all down?! I decided right then and there I would write a book describing the journey I took to become a jester.

That very evening, before I sat down in front of the computer to begin, I went out and bought a pointy, multicolored cap.

The very next morning, I found myself sitting at my desk wearing my jester's cap, ready to begin. I smiled. This was going to be fun!

In that moment I had little idea that my own journey was only beginning and that emails from my mysterious friend would resume in the months ahead. That, however, is a tale for the next book.

Creating and Fostering Jestership in Your Organization

As you turned these pages, I hope you had some insights about yourself as a potential jester. You may have already started to use the stories to get a sense of where blind spots may exist around you. If you have discovered some truth, and are ready to take action, I applaud you! What next? The future of your jester journey, if you are willing, now involves personal commitment.

The jester philosophy can be adopted in three distinct but complementary ways:

- It can be a philosophy an individual commits to in order to further his or her *own* abilities and growth: an internal jester. With this commitment, the jester is consistently looking for and addressing blind spots in his or her own perspectives. She or he continuously enlists others to help uncover their own blind spots even though those enlisted may never hear the word "jester" uttered in public. This philosophy can work wonderfully if you feel like you exist in an environment that would completely reject the idea of jestership. These jesters keep their caps hidden in a drawer under file folders and a stapler.

- It can also be a philosophy an individual commits to in order to further *another's* abilities and growth: an external jester for others. This is the role of the traditional jester of ancient China who provided a voice when no one else would speak. With this commitment the jester is consistently addressing blind spots in him- or herself, colleagues, and the leadership within his or her organization. This involves applying the skills needed to discern blind spots but also the techniques needed to subtly assist others in noticing and addressing them. These jesters get very good at understanding when and where jestership is appropriate and who it may be acceptable to. These jesters wear their caps in public ... but not all of the time.

- Finally, jestership can be a philosophy committed to by a group of people (or an entire organization!) in order to further *the entire group's* abilities and growth. This is the most exciting environment to be in because each jester is surrounded by other jesters. With this commitment, each person takes responsibility and accountability to create and maintain an ongoing culture of jestership within the group. As a team, they consistently look for and address blind spots in the perspectives of the other members. Individuals are committed to uncovering as many as they can for others, and to taking ownership and addressing the personal blind spots others point out. They hold each other accountable to adopt and maintain true jester attitude and behavior. These jesters wear their caps at all times.

Which way of looking at jestership is right for you? The answer depends on your circumstances, your ability to commit, and your organization's readiness to hear what a true jester might have to say.

I suggest you think of the three stages as stepping stones. Concentrate first on becoming an internal jester. Become skilled at illuminating and addressing your own blind spots. Go back through the book, re-read the e-mails, and spend some time with each of the stories. Contemplate what they might mean for you, and plan actions to involve others in gathering information and insight about those areas that you may have blindness in. Address the blind spots you uncover.

Commit to taking on this internal role and, as your own blind spots fall away, you will start to shine within your organization without ever having to have talked about "jestership." People will be astounded by your abilities, insights, and understanding. Soon, some will come to you to ask how you do it. At that point you can move on to the next stage and step into the role of a jester for others.

Moving to this step involves taking a more open and active role as a jester in your organization. This could involve speaking your mind more often, speaking up for those that choose not to, challenging the status quo and illuminating the blind spots you uncover in more public ways. Remember to use your jester skills to perform all of the above with subtlety, creativity, and grace because this role can be very tricky—even dangerous if entered into haphazardly. Choose when to step into the role of jester carefully as you begin. It may be a little daunting at first, but the more you do it, the better you will get at it and the more people will expect it from you! Eventually, if you make your presence known slowly and carefully, you may gain a great, unique reputation in your organization!

As an example, take Paul Birch and his role within British Airways (BA). During his career with the airline, Paul had his hand in most everything at one time or another. "Every time I was ready to retire," he recalls, "my boss would say, 'I've got an interesting job for you.' Finally, I announced that it was time for me to go. He said, 'What would it take to keep you?'" Inspired by an article on the character of the fool in *King Lear*, Birch wrote a job description for a jester. He thought this role would be for someone who would question authority, promote honesty, and approach problems in creative ways.

In response, in 1995, BA appointed Paul Birch the company's official "corporate jester." If Paul gave you one of his business cards at that time you saw that the company wasn't kidding; his unique title was prominently displayed.

What followed was an experiment with amazing results. During his tenure in the position Paul gave pointers to top executives on how to be less confrontational, made suggestions about the design and layout of the company's headquarters, challenged status quo standards and said things that most other people inside the company were afraid to say. As a result, Paul guided the company in illuminating and addressing countless blind spots.

Your organization may not be quite ready to appoint an official corporate jester, but there may be more support for jestership than you think. Start with your commitment to internal jestership and begin to provide jestership for those who come to you, and eventually you will see something interesting occur. As more and more people gather around you and adopt your jester perspective, jester-like thought and behavior will spread throughout the organization. At some point, if enough people adopt the paradigm, you will see a shift in the actual organizational culture! One day you will look around the organization and notice jestership everywhere.

People will be more likely to be honest and open in discussions. Staff will be more forthcoming in sharing perspectives that differ from those of "management." Your colleagues will be open to feedback and ready to aggressively address blind spots others help them discover. You will walk around the organization wondering just what happened. The truth is ... YOU happened.

Soon after, the concept of jestership may become a cultural norm in your organization. You should make sure this is pointed out, labeled, and enshrined. Newcomers into the organization need to understand what it is and those who have not completely adopted it need to see it as a cultural expectation. Very soon, you will have a long-lasting, self-sustaining organization full of jesters. These kind of places are rare, interesting, and fun environments—and they are extremely successful. Organizations that reach this stage are something special to behold. You can start constructing one today.

So ... are you ready? Put on your multicolored cap and begin your own jestership journey. See where it takes you.

Good luck! Enjoy making a difference.

An Invitation

I cordially invite you visit www.corporatejester.com.

At the website you can contact me, order more copies of this book, read more about the concept of jestership, see suggestions for further reading, meet others who have started their jestership journeys, and take a look at the services and products we provide for individuals and organizations.

The site also has a special section for readers of this book.

I look forward to hearing from you.

David Riveness

Bibliography

Aesop. **The Complete Fables.** Penguin Classics, new edition (March 1, 1998); ISBN: 0140446494.

Brothers Grimm. **The Complete Brothers Grimm Fairy Tales.** Gramercy (May 9, 1993); ISBN: 051709293X.

Disney Storybook Collection. Disney Press, 1st ed. (September 1, 1998); ISBN: 0786832347.

Durant, Will. **The Story of Civilization: Part II, The Life of Greece.** Simon and Schuster, 1939.

Exploratorium educational website. **Blind Spot.** Available at: http://www.exploratorium.edu/snacks/blind_spot.html. Accessed Oct. 2005.

Feynman, Richard P. **What Do You Care What Other People Think?: Further Adventures of a Curious Character.** Bantam (October 1, 1989); ISBN: 0553347845.

Harvey, Jerry B. **The Abilene Paradox and Other Meditations on Management.** Jossey-Bass, new edition (August 9, 1996); ISBN: 0787902772.

Freiberg, Kevin and Freiberg, Jackie. **Nuts! Southwest Airlines' Crazy Recipe for Business and Personal Success.** Broadway, reprint edition (February 17, 1998); ISBN: 0767901843.

Sittenfeld, Curtis. **He's No Fool (But He Plays One inside Companies)**. Fast Company; November 1988: 66.

About the Author

David T. Riveness is the founder and current CEO of *Corporate Jester*, a company focused on personal and organizational development. David develops and delivers personalized keynote speeches, organizes learning sessions and provides high-achievement coaching for companies, organizations, and individuals.

Prior to founding Corporate Jester, David served as the Director of Global Facilitations for Eagle's Flight, a world-wide innovator in the development and delivery of practical training programs for organizations. While at Eagle's Flight, he facilitated and implemented training programs for such industry leaders as Warner Bros., NIKE, ESPN, Pfizer, The American Heart Association, and Citibank on a variety of topics relating to organizational and individual effectiveness. David has successfully facilitated dynamic training workshops and speaking engagements ranging in scale from intimate, classroom-style forums to large-scale, formal presentations with over 3,500 attendees.

His experiences have been global in scope; David has facilitated and spoken across the world, including such diverse locations as India, China, Brazil and the Czech Republic.

Further complementing his leadership experience, David has worked in the academic arena, both in teaching and management capacities at a number of colleges and universities.

David received his M.A. from Bowling Green University and holds a B.A. from Cal Poly State University. He is a member of the International Coach Federation (IFC), the National Speaker's Association (NSA), and the American Society for Training and Development (ASTD).

When he's not traveling the world to share the jester concept with others, Dave splits his time between Los Angeles and San Miguel de Allende, a small town in central Mexico.

Are you ready to bring the Secrets of the Corporate Jester into your organization?

Looking for a dynamic, fun and interesting keynote speaker for your next conference?

Interested in acquiring multiple copies of the Secret Jester for colleagues?

Searching for a training program that incorporates Jestership learning?

For more information about any of the above, or to chat about something clever we haven't thought about yet, email us at info@corporatejester.com or email Dave directly at driveness@corporatejester.com. We would love to hear from you!

Pick up a copy of the business book that is changing the way people perceive organizations.

"I truly enjoyed the book.... Developing an ability to eliminate blind spots, our own or those of others, is essential for success in every business."
David Steinhart, Learning Consultant

"... a fun and intriguing read filled with insights into what it takes to be a successful leader in today's complex corporate environments."
Mary Peery, Senior VP, Hewlett Packard

"The concept offered a realistic way to overcome leadership shortcomings. I could see this as a successful training tool. I liked it!"
Dean Parker, Senior VP, Great Central Insurance

"Every person that wants to influence culture change and build leadership in any organization should give this a read."
Doug Bryant, VP, Advance Auto Parts

"... a totally unique and really outstanding way for the reader to look at organizational culture and leadership."
William Cooper, Reader Views

The Secret Life of the Corporate Jester is available now in hardback and softcover at www.corporatejester.com, www.amazon.com, and selected bookstores.

Printed in the United States
98580LV00003B/139-201/A